We Declare!

Songs, Chants, Dances, and Multimedia Projects

by
Merrill Collins

Lyrics from

Towards a Global Ethic: An Initial Declaration

for All Ages

We Declare!
Songs, Chants, Dances and Multimedia Projects

ISBN: 978-09748341-1-5

© Merrill Collins 2022

Photography by Yvon Chausseblanche

Published by Spiraling Music (ASCAP)
1236 Sherman St. #1
Alameda, CA 94501
www.spiralingmusic.com

*Get the companion soundtrack to this book of scores and curricula
everywhere streaming music is available, or at
www.spiralingmusic.com*

Dedicated
to

"The community of living beings,
the community of life."

— from the song, *We are Interdependent*

Based on
Towards a Global Ethic:
*An Initial Declaration of the
Parliament of the World's Religions*

PALM LEAF
RATTLE
from India

Foreword by Kabir Sehgal

The World's Fair in Chicago in 1893 has a special place in my heart.

That might sound odd or even random.

But I grew up hearing about this event, which was organized by Judge Charles Carroll of the Supreme Court. It was a formal gathering of religious leaders from Eastern and Western spiritual traditions.

It was there that an Indian monk delivered a speech for the ages.

Swami Vivekananda spoke about the power of tolerance, and how it's necessary to eschew fanaticism.

His speech rippled around the world and over the generations.

Many Indians consider this speech a major moment of global import.

Years later, a council was formed, which produced a groundbreaking document: "Towards a Global Ethic: An Initial Declaration" that built on the monk's speech.

This declaration reflected the common ground shared by the world's religious and spiritual traditions.

Common ground. It almost sounds quaint in the turbulent times in which we live. But it's a message that is profound and powerful.

The book that's in your hands is borne of this same spirit of coming together – and common humanity.

It's important that individuals and institutions that constitute our civil society have an ethical compass that guides proper decision making. Among the traits that we should all embody include – expressing love and understanding non-violence.

What makes this project special is Merrill Collins' art, which ultimately makes these pages more accessible, professional, and beautiful. Music brings us together. And throughout this journey you'll discover how the creative spirit can guide us to
higher ground.

-Kabir Sehgal

Kabir Sehgal is a bestselling author who has produced over 80 albums and won seven Grammy & five Latin Grammy Awards, including works with John Lewis, Deepak Chopra, and Paul Avgerinos.

CASTANET from China

Contents

Acknowledgments iv
Introduction v

Towards a Global Ethic: An Initial Declaration 1

Projects

    We Are Interdependent (Track 1) 3

    Golden Rules Ceremony (Track 2) 7

    Forsaking Violence (Track 3) 11

    Humankind Is Our Family (Track 4) 15

    We Are Interdependent - Ethno-Trance Dance (Track 5) 19

    Opening Our Hearts (Track 6) 20

    We The Peoples Public Service Announcements (Track 7-12) ..25

    Cause and Effect (Track 8) 27

Appendices 31

    I. Global Ethic Resources 32

    II. World Instrument Resources 33

    III. How to Use the Soundtrack 34

    IV. Minor Release Form for Video 35

Index 36
The Artists 37

Turtle OCARINA from Mexico

Acknowledgements

I express special appreciation to the people whose participation has helped shape these projects:

- Rev. Stephen Avino, Executive Director, and Dr. Myriam Renaud, Director of Global Ethic Project, of the Parliament of the World's Religions for permission to reprint the text of *Towards a Global Ethic: An Initial Declaration*.

- Dr. Professor Hans Küng and Dr. Günther Gebhart of the Global Ethic Foundation for encouragement on development of these pieces.

- Nushin Mavaddit and Anne Perry whose invitation to present these works at the Association of Baha'i Studies Conference 2003 led to the creation of this book.

- Mary Sano, original choreographer, whose collaboration in 1995 helped identify the concepts of the text and ways to create interaction.

- Artists Toward a Global Ethic 1996 - 1999 whose participation in these projects gave voice to the audio CD, *We the Peoples Public Service Announcements*. Thank you to the artists who gave presentations in Capetown South Africa at the Council for the Parliament of the Worlds Religions Conference in 1999: John Donovan, Maria Chapital, Satoko Woodcock, Lizzy Cole, Chris Ray Collins and Blake Rains. Thank you also to Kevin Dusek, Daryl Keyes, Pope Flyne, Joseph Hebert, Dan Ross, Melissa Renati-Wong, Charles Moselle and all of my artist friends and family.

- Paul Chaffee and the Interfaith Center at the Presidio in San Francisco.

- Tiffany Puett, Assistant Director, Temple of Understanding, for sharing list of Golden Rules.

- Movement of Spiritual Inner Awareness, www.msia.org, for teachings on Hu and Ani-Hu chants.

- Leanna James and Northern California Ministers of M.S.I.A.

- Jim Costanzo, Mrs. Sams, and the children of the Piedmont Avenue Child Development Center who have participated in developing these projects.

- Kristen Caven for co-creativity, graphics and book design; Karl Pister for score design and preparation.

- Fatima Yousuf and Piedmont Copy for graphic design.

- Edward Jones of Onyx and Opal, Oakland, world instruments resources.

- Clara Hsu of the Clarion Music Center in San Francisco, world instruments resources.

- Marilyn Nebolsky of Global Exchange, Berkeley, world instruments resources.

- Marjorie Lambert and LeAnna Sharp, proof reading

- Yvon Chausseblanche for photography and support in holding the vision.

— *Merrill Collins*

Native American PEACE FLUTE

Introduction

We Declare! is a collection of interactive music projects based on *Towards a Global Ethic: An Initial Declaration*, the signature document of the Parliament of the World's Religions since 1993. Primarily written by Hans Küng at the behest of the Parliament, this widely collaborative document expresses the basic moral principles shared by people throughout the world, whether religious or not. Instructions, lyrics, score and educational materials (Sounds of the World) are provided with each of the various projects.

These projects were composed with the intention of bringing this text to life as an accessible cultural expression. Generated at the grassroots level, these works have been designed to be used intergenerationally in schools, preschools, youth groups and senior centers, as well as at intercultural, interfaith and social justice events. They were cited at the 1999 World Religions conference in CapeTown, South Africa, as "Gifts of Service to the World."

As international literacy becomes more crucial, so does the understanding of values shared by all humankind. These interactive music projects offer creatively engaging ways for performers and audiences alike to celebrate the ideas that unite us all. Participants in each project not only build community, but build an understanding of the foundations of community.

Using this book in conjunction with the instrumental recordings, teachers and activities directors who wish to create performances for school assemblies, civic events, and community gatherings can easily prepare presentations. Most of these projects are designed for a cantor or lead singer and an assembly of children and/or adults. Some can also be choreographed. Ideas for art and multimedia are included in the instructions. Special instructions are also included for non-musicians.

Another theme of this collection is the use of instruments from indigenous cultures around the world. The instructions for each project are illustrated with pictures of these instruments in a "Sounds of the World" music lesson. These various drums, shakers and bells can be heard on the CD and may also be played along live to the soundtrack if available. Music educators will find this a perfect introduction to World Music.

Fish-shaped WOOD BLOCK from Thailand

The Source of Song Lyrics

Hans Küng with Kofi Annan

Towards a Global Ethic: An Initial Declaration

"A common ethic...within all the religious teachings of the world...can supply the moral foundation for a vision to lead men and women away from despair, and society away from chaos."

— *Hans Küng, President of the Foundation for a Global Ethic (Stiftung Weltethos)*

"Universal values are...more acutely needed, in this age of globalization, than ever before. Every society needs to be bound together by common values, so that its members know what to expect of each other, and have some shared principles by which to manage their differences without resorting to violence.... That is true of local communities and of national communities. Today, as globalization brings us all closer together, and our lives are affected almost instantly by things that people say and do on the far side of the world, we also feel the need to live as a global community. And we can do so only if we have global values to bind us together."

—*Kofi Annan, Former UN Secretary General,
in his Global Ethic Lecture at the University of Tübingen, 2003*

This excerpt from Towards a Global Ethic: An Initial Declaration was written by Thomas Baima and Daniel Gómez-Ibáñez.

GHUNGAROOS
from India

We Declare:

We are interdependent. Each of us depends on the well-being of the whole, and so we have respect for the community of living beings, for people, animals, and plants, and for the preservation of Earth, the air, water and soil.

We take individual responsibility for all we do. All our decisions, actions, and failures to act have consequences.

We must treat others as we wish others to treat us. We make a commitment to respect life and dignity, individuality and diversity, so that every person is treated humanely, without exception. We must have patience, and acceptance. We must be able to forgive, learning from the past but never allowing ourselves to be enslaved by memories of hate. Opening our hearts to one another, we must sink our narrow differences for the cause of the world community, practicing a culture of solidarity and relatedness.

We consider humankind our family. We must strive to be kind and generous. We must not live for ourselves alone, but should also serve others, never forgetting the children, the aged, the poor, the suffering, the disabled, the refugees, and the lonely. No person should ever be considered or treated as a second-class citizen, or be exploited in any way whatsoever. There should be equal partnership between men and women. We must not commit any kind of sexual immorality. We must put behind us all forms of domination and abuse.

We commit ourselves to a culture of non-violence, respect, justice, and peace. We shall not oppress, injure, torture, or kill other human beings, forsaking violence as a means of settling differences.

We must strive for a just social and economic order, in which everyone has an equal chance to reach full potential as a human being. We must speak and act truthfully and with compassion, dealing fairly with all, and avoiding prejudice and hatred. We must not steal.

We must move beyond the dominance of greed for power, prestige, money, and consumption to make a just and peaceful world.

Earth cannot be changed for the better unless the consciousness of individuals is changed first. We pledge to increase our awareness by disciplining our minds, by meditation, by prayer, or by positive thinking. Without risk and a readiness to sacrifice there can be no fundamental change in our situation. Therefore we commit ourselves to this global ethic, to understanding one another, and to socially beneficial, peace-fostering, and nature-friendly ways of life.

We invite all people, whether religious or not, to do the same.

ELEPHANT BELLS

At the end of the of the track, the Gankoqui bell sings its own, two-toned rhythmic motif, and is joined by a family of Elephant Bells from India.

SOUNDS OF THE WORLD

ELEPHANT BELLS
from India

CHA-CHAS

Cha-chas are ankle bracelets which make rhythmic sounds as we move our feet. Pope Flyne, the master African drummer who plays on track 1, wears a unique combination of cha-chas when he performs:

1) Ghungaroos, small brass bells from India (a spiral of ghungaroos is shown on previous page)

2) Goat hooves from Bolivia (shown at left)

Wearing cha-chas on the feet can help participants count (left-right) the 14 measure introduction of this song, and the 20 measure segment leading into the final refrain.

CHA-CHAS
from Bolivia

We Are Interdependent

Track 1 - 5:11

This project illuminates an idea from the Global Ethic document through art, music and the many languages of a diverse community.

Instructions:

1) Translate: Find out what languages are represented by various project participants and their families. Collect translations of the phrase,

"Each of us depends on the well-being of the whole."

Have participants practice pronouncing the line.

2) Illustrate: Write the phrase down and illustrate it. Create a bulletin board, banners, postcards, or other visual media.

3) Add Instruments: Suggested for this piece: gankoqui bell, elephant bells, ankle bells ("ghungaroos"), ankle shakers ("cha-chas").

4) Celebrate: For the performance, display all the artwork. The lead singer sings the refrain, then invites the assembly to repeat. Speakers take turns offering the one-line translations in verse 3. These speakers may line up on stage or at a microphone to deliver their lines.

GANKOQUI
from Ghana

A Gankoqui is a two-toned bell (the name indicating parent/child) from Ghana, which can be heard on the CD leading into each refrain, signaling a rhythmic alert.

Skills Involved	Age Group	Recommended Preparaton Time	Presentation Time
• singing • counting with feet • collecting and pronouncing multiple languages • art	3-5 6-10 11-14 15 to adult	4 weeks 3 weeks 2 weeks 1-2 weeks	5:08 minutes

We Are Interdependent

Lyrics

Refrain:
We are interdependent
We are interdependent
We are interdependent
Chacun et chacune

Verse 1:
In the community of living beings
In the community of life
In the community of people, plants and animals,
In the community of life

(refrain)

Verse 2:
And for the preservation of the earth
And of the water, soil and air
And for the preservation of the earth
And of the water, soil and air

(refrain)

Verse 3:
Each of us depends on the well-being of the whole. (Repeat)

Invite your group to speak this line in a variety of languages.

A few examples:

French: Chacun et chacune d'entre nous dépend du bien-être de l'ensemble.
Spanish: Cada uno de nosotros depende de la bienestar del conjunto.
Tagalog: Lahat tayo uma-asa sa kabutihan nang bawat isa.
German: Jede und jeder von uns hängt vom Wohlergehen des Ganzen ab.
Italian: Ognuno di noi dipende dai benessedsre della totalita.
Urdu: ہر کوئی سب اچھا ہو نے کی اُمید پر قائم ہے۔

Add your own: _____

_____

_____

_____

Excerpt from Towards A Global Ethic: An Initial Declaration

"We are interdependent. Each of us depends on the well-being of the whole, and so we have respect for the community of living beings, for people, animals, and plants, and for the preservation of the Earth, the air, water and soil."

Text reprinted with permission from the Parliament of the World's Religions (www.parliamentofreligions.org)

TINGSHA BELLS from Tibet

SOUNDS OF THE WORLD

TINGSHA BELLS

These bells come from Tibet and India. They work well in the Golden Rules Ceremony when played after each reading. A leader of the ceremony may use them to queue the assembly when to come back in on the refrain after each set of readings.

Tingsha bells are micro-tonal and rich in high overtones. These bells offer an immediate lesson in World music, when we realize that the entire world does not always break down the octave into 12 equal tones such as Western music.

When shopping for Tingsha bells, bring along a pitch reference, such as a pitch pipe or tuning fork to help identify the pitch of the bell. The Golden Rules Ceremony is in the key of A Major, as we know keys in western music. Harmonious tones for complimentary tingsha bells would sound the root note, A, or the dominant pitch, E.

RAIN STICKS

Rain sticks hail from more than one indigenous peoples. In South America rain sticks are used in ceremonies to bring rain to the desert. Rain sticks are tubular, made either from wood skeletons of dead cactus plants or bamboo. The branches are hollowed out and filled with pebbles or grains of varying size. To play a rain stick, tilt it slowly and become aware of the speed of the falling pebbles inside. When all the pebbles have fallen to the bottom, turn it slowly upside down again. Variations on the sound can be created by twisting the stick while tilting it, and by exploring different angles of tilt. When more than one rainstick is played, the sound can be continuous. It is possible to make rain sticks as a craft project. (Please see Resources Appendix II).

RAIN STICKS from Chile

Golden Rules Ceremony

Track 2 - 10:18

This ceremony presents and celebrates the concept of the Golden Rules as they appear in different religions.

BRASS CHINESE BELLS

Instructions:
Invite volunteer readers from the group. The lead singer begins with the chant. Speakers present each reading. Repeat the refrain after each four readings. The "Ani-Hu" chant may be sung softly by a chorus underscoring the text.

Add Instruments:
Suggested for this piece: Tingsha bells and rain sticks.

sanskrit "HU"

Ani-Hu

The Ani-Hu chant combines the ancient Sanskrit syllables, A-NI, which invokes the quality of empathy, with the syllable HU, an ancient name for Spirit.

Composer's Notes:

"When we did this piece at a preliminary conference to the CPWR Conference in Capetown, South Africa, in 1999, I invited twelve volunteers from the audience to do the spoken readings. People in the room were gathered from all over the world and were getting acquainted. Although the readings are easy to vocalize, a lively discussion preceded the start of the music as the volunteers asked each other how to pronounce the text sources. Later, once the music got going, the beauty of the experience for me was listening to the unique tone of each reader's voice, making the composition a collage of international sounds."

Skills Involved	Age Group	Recommended Preparaton Time	Presentation Time
• singing • reading • research, asking questions • speaking • pronouncing • uncommon words • memorization, recitation	3-5 6-10 11-14 15 to adult	4 weeks 2 weeks 1 weeks 1/2 hour	5-10 minutes depending on number of readings

WE DECLARE! • Golden Rules Ceremony • Track 2

Golden Rules Ceremony

Lyrics

Refrain

"We treat others as we wish to be treated."

Chant

"Ani-Hu"

A sacred chant to invoke empathy may be sung over the ceremonial music.

Spoken Readings:

1) Baha'i Faith: "Lay not on any soul which ye would not wish to be laid upon you, and desire not for any one the things ye would not desire for yourselves." (Baha'u'llah)

2) Buddhism: "Hurt not others in ways that you yourself would find hurtful." (Udana-Varga, 5:18)

3) Christianity: "In everything, do to others as you would have them do to you; for this is the law and the prophets." (Matthew 7:12 - NRSV)

4) Confucianism: "Do not unto others what you would not have them do unto you." (Analects 15:23)

Repeat Refrain and Chant:

5) Hinduism: "This is the sum of duty: do naught unto others which would cause you pain if done to you." (Mahabharata 5:1517)

6) Islam: "No one of you is a believer until he desires for his brother that which he desires for himself." (Sunnab)

7) Jainism: "In happiness and suffering, in joy and grief, we should regard all creatures as we regard our own self." (Lord Mahavir 24th Tirthankara)

8) Judaism: "What is hateful to you, do not to your fellow human beings. That is the law; all the rest is commentary." (Talmud, Shabbat 31a)

Repeat Refrain and Chant:

9) Native American: "Respect for all life is the foundation." (The Great Law of Peace)

10) Sikhism: "Don't create enmity with anyone, as God is within everyone." (Guru Arjan Devji 259. Guru Granth Sahib)

11) Zoroastrianism: "That nature is good only when it shall do unto another whatsoever is not good for its own self." (Dadistan-i-Dinik 94.3)

12) Add your own: _____

13) Final Reading: "We must treat others as we wish others to treat us. We make a commitment to respect life and dignity, individuality and diversity, so that every person is treated humanely, without exception. We must have patience, and acceptance. We must be able to forgive, learning from the past but never allowing ourselves to be enslaved by memories of hate. Opening our hearts to one another, we must sink our narrow differences for the cause of the world community, practicing a culture of solidarity and relatedness."

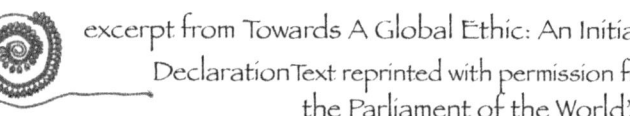

excerpt from Towards A Global Ethic: An Initial Declaration Text reprinted with permission from the Parliament of the World's Religionss

SOUNDS OF THE WORLD

Dragonfly from Nicaragua

Frog from Vietnam

Duck from Mexico

"Make a just and peaceful world with nature friendly ways of life".

OCARINAS

Ocarinas are one of the most ancient instruments in the world, created by humans as a way of imitating the calls of doves, and thus engage in the dove's conversation. They are made of clay and come in many shapes. Ocarinas are fitting to this piece, especially during section D.

RASPS

From Vietnam, hand carved wooden instruments shaped like frogs, grasshoppers, and turtles, make sounds to imitate and talk to these creatures. These instruments, played by stroking with a stick, represent sounds heard in nature, and can be added also to "Forsaking Violence".

Forsaking Violence

Track 3 - 6:03

> *A community meditation on non-violence that may include dance.*

Instructions:

Begin with a reading of the text. Collaboratively create a dance or movement to express each idea. A cantor leads, with the assembly repeating each segment.

Add Instruments:
Suggested for this piece: nature sounds, ocarinas, flutes, recorders, gong, rasps.

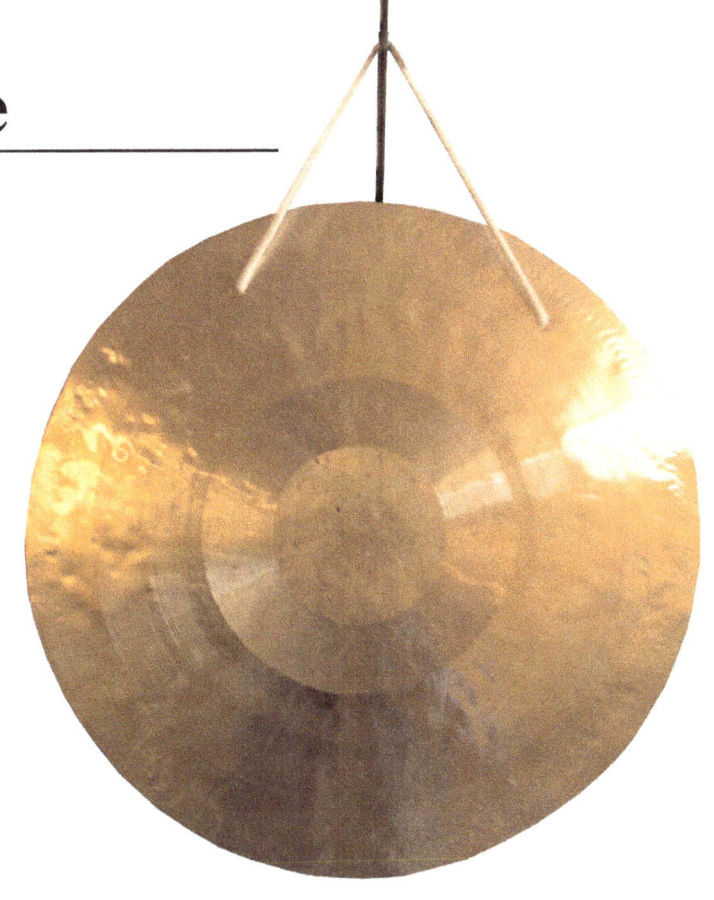

GONG

Most commonly found in China and Indonesia, gongs have a ceremonial place in ritual and celebration. In the piece "Forsaking Violence" a gong may be struck at the climactic point of the phrase, "As a means of settling differences". It is appropriate at the end of this piece to walk through the assembly and strike a gong in leading the spoken mantra, "We commit ourselves".

Choreographer's Notes:

"One way of choreographing this piece is to work with the song and find the movements which depict the meaning of the words. If you can express with the gestures and movements how you feel about violence in your experience, this could be a great dance piece for everyone. Choreographing this was a fun experience for me. I danced the opening parts in a red tunic as a solo, bringing in a circle of dancers in white for 'make a just and peaceful world.' We danced in counterpoint as the two themes 'no violence please' and 'make a just and peaceful world' were sung simultaneously. As we all exited, the audience joined us in the spoken chant, 'we commit ourselves.'"

—Mary Sano
Original choreographer for the 50th anniversary of the United Nations, San Francisco events

"We Commit Ourselves"

Skills Involved	Age Group	Recommended Preparaton Time	Presentation Time
• Singing • Movement • Commitment	3-5 6-10 11-14 15 to adult	4 weeks 2-4 weeks 2 weeks 1 week	6 to 10 minutes

Forsaking Violence

Lyrics

 Excerpt from Towards A Global Ethic: An Initial Declaration

"We commit ourselves to a culture of non-violence, respect, justice, and peace. We shall not oppress, injure, torture, or kill other human beings, forsaking violence as a means of settling differences. Make a just and peaceful world, with nature-friendly ways of life."

Text reprinted with permission from the Parliament of the World's Religions (www.parliamentofreligions.org)

Begin this piece with a reading of the spoken text.

Cantor:	No violence, please. No violence, please. No violence, please. No violence, please. No violence, please. No violence, please.	**A**
Assembly:	No violence, please. No violence, please. No violence, please. No violence, please. No violence, please. No violence, please.	**A**
Cantor:	Forsaking violence. Forsaking violence. Forsaking violence. Forsaking violence.	**B**
Assembly:	Forsaking violence. Forsaking violence. Forsaking violence. Forsaking violence.	**B**
All:	As a means of settling differences.	**C**

Repeat the entire chant **A B C** *three times.*

All:	Make a just and peaceful world with nature-friendly ways of life.	**D**

Repeat **D** *eight times.*

All:	We commit ourselves.	**E**

Repeat ad lib.

SOUNDS OF THE WORLD

BELLS

Bells are found all over the world in every culture. They come in many shapes and sizes and are often found in groups, from Bell Trees to the Gamelan. Bells also have a ceremonial sound to them that creates a tonal space to focus minds for a special moment.

Bells can be added as a complimentary live sound to this piece when played sensitively. The bells heard on this recording were selected for their tonal matching qualities. Singing Bowls from Tibet (see page 17) have a unique quality when played as an ongoing tone. (See Resources for information on how to play Singing Bowls.) "Humankind Is Our Family" revolves around the pitch, F.

Composer's Notes
*When I first wrote **Humankind Is Our Family**, my wish was to pass out bells for every member of the assembly to play. Unfortunately, this was beyond my budget. However, I have since attended events where people bring bells from home. This could be a "B.Y.O.B." (Bring Your Own Bell) performance piece.*

GLASS HARMONICA

Glasses can be filled with water to create specific pitches when rubbed with a moist finger around the rim. This sound can be heard on the CD, and can certainly be added live along with the vocal chant, "Hu." Experiment with the amount of water in a glass until you get a perfect "F" pitch. Crystal works best.

MINI-COW BELLS from India

GOBLET filled with H2o

Humankind is Our Family

Track 4 - 6:04

A multi-media experience celebrating the diversity of humanity.

Instructions:

Create visual art about all the different races, and display it in a harmonious way while playing the music and speaking the concept.

Visual Art
The music on this track is intended to be a soundtrack for a visual multi-media presentation. The visual presentation may be projected photographs and /or handmade artwork depicting peoples of every race, or a combination. The group doing the project is encouraged to bring pictures of themselves and their immediate family members. Images of these familiar faces would then be shown in alternation with images of peoples elsewhere on the globe. Collages should include as many varieties of people as can be found. The music is very reflective, and the change rate of the images should likewise be unhurried.

Add Instruments:
Singing bowl, bell, bell tree, glass harmonica, marimba, xylophone.

Presentation Ideas
This piece has a lot of subtlety and can presented as a performance at an assembly, but also works well as a background piece in public places such as lobbies of buildings, airports, art galleries, or hallways where people gather for events, setting an over-all tone of acceptance and connection.

This is a chant layered on a single tone, sung as **Hu** on the note-F. One person memorizes the complete quotation and recites it during the chant. An assembly may join in with the lead chant singer.

BELL TREE from Japan

Skills Involved	Age Group	Recommended Preparaton Time	Presentation Time
• Creating artwork • Collecting images • Photography • Media preparation • Singing • Recitation	3-5 6-10 11-14 15 to adult	1 week 4 hours 3 hours 3-10 hours	6 minutes (may be repeated)

Humankind Is Our Family

Lyrics

Hu Chant

Cantor: *Hu*
Assembly: *Hu*

Cantor: *Human*
Assembly: *Human*

Cantor: *Humankind*
Assembly: *Humankind*

Cantor: *Humankind is our family*
Assembly: *Humankind is our family*

 Excerpt from Towards A Global Ethic: An Initial Declaration

"We consider humankind our family. We do not live for ourselves alone, but also serving others, never forgetting the children, the aged, the poor, the suffering, the disabled, the refugees, and the lonely."

Text reprinted with permission from the Parliament of the World's Religions (www.parliamentofreligions.org)

Hu

"Hu" is an ancient sound found in Sanskrit, Hebrew, and Tibetan traditions that is intoned as an invocation. "Hu" is the first sound of the word "Human." This universal chant was the initial blessing of the Interfaith Chapel in San Francisco, sung a capella with bells.

Composer's Notes:

We sang this chant as the prelude to a twilight retreat led by Dom Lawrence Freeman, O.S.B., and Ajahn Amaro, hosted by the United Religions Initiative on May 6, 1997. I asked my nephew to memorize the excerpt. We had a week to prepare. Everyday as we walked back from the grocery store he practiced the recitation, counting the seven population groups on his fingers. Naturally we also discussed the meaning of the quote. Several people at the event remarked about the poignancy of having a child do the recitation. Not only is the voice of a child pure over the sound of the Hu chant, the opportunity to include a young person models for the community the ideals of interfaith education.

SINGING BOWL from Tibet

We Declare!

Humankind Is Our Family

Dedicated to my nephew, James Patrick Manus

Starti

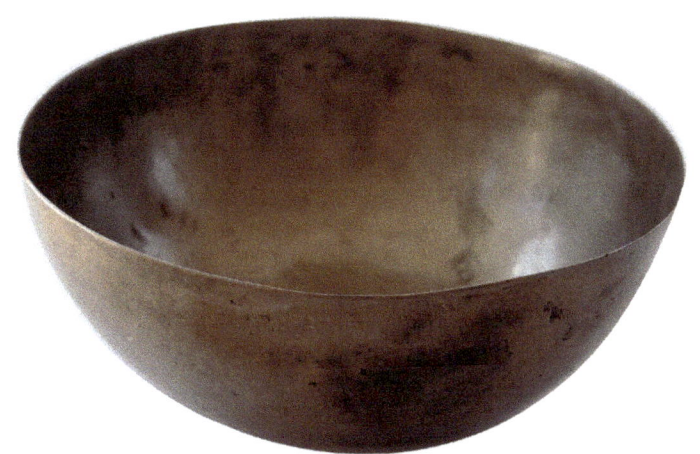

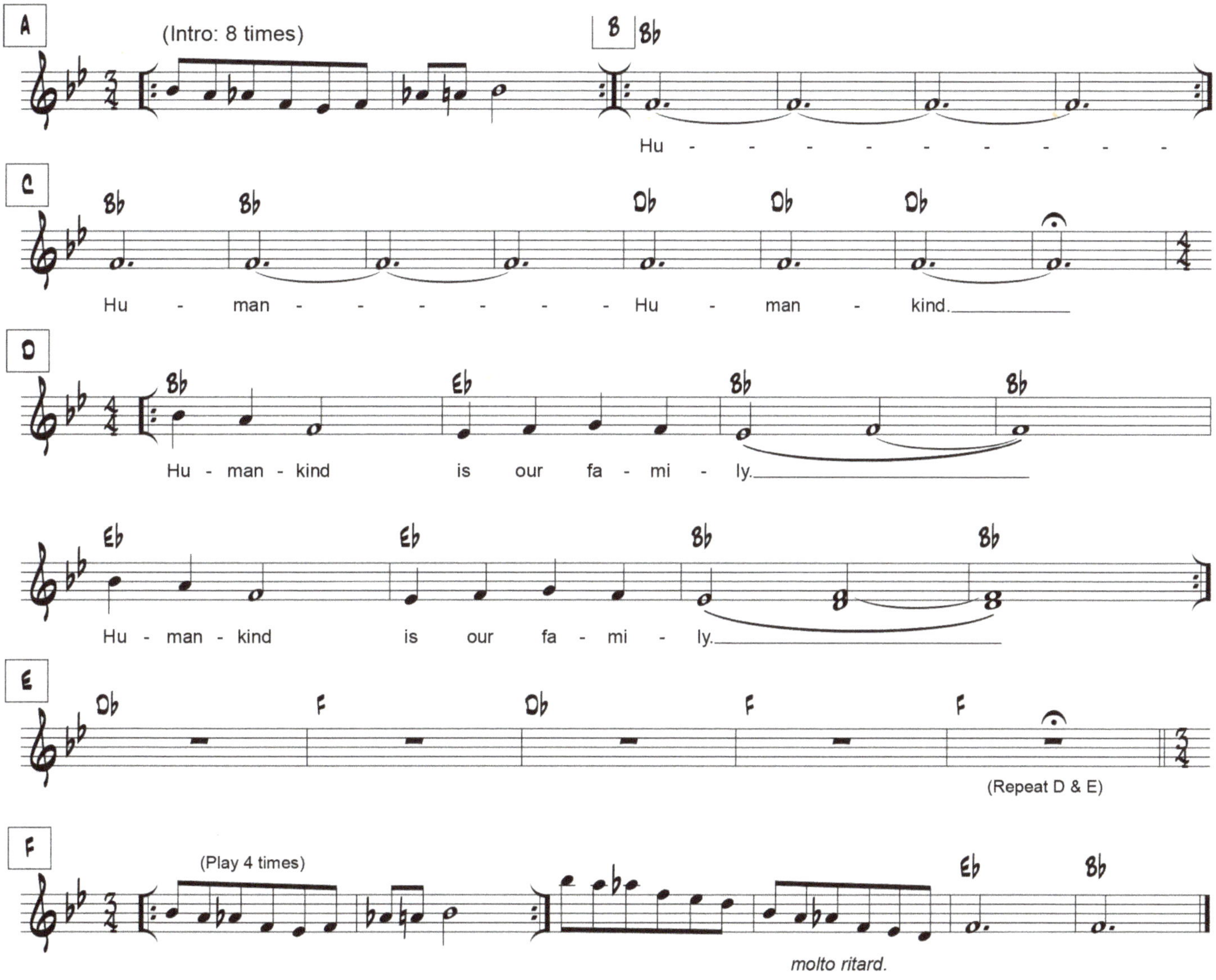

On the recording the sequence is A (8x), B (2x), C (1x), D (2x), E (1x), D (2x), E (1x), F (1x)

SOUNDS OF THE WORLD

DIJIRI-DOO from Australia

DIJIRI-DOO

Traditional dijiri-doos are made from trees hollowed by termites and burning coals. One end is blocked by wax, and the instrument is played by blowing with relaxed lips on the other end. The sound of the dijiri-doo (or didgeridu -- there are many spellings) is a long, low buzzing song that requires meditative lung control. The music of Australian Aboriginals carries for miles across the dry air of the Outback desert.

Musically, dijiri-doos provide a droning sound, which is made in other cultures by the hurdy-gurdy, bagpipes, Indian harmonium, or even a pipe organ with the pedal held down. The vocal drone of Tibetan Monks is also a unique sound. The musical function of the drone is to provide a harmonic base, to hold the bottom tone while other melodies play over the top. Some call the drone sound "the ground."

KULING-TANG

This traditional Philippine instrument is a series of eight enormous, pot-shaped bells arranged harmonically, and usually played by an ensemble of percussionists and dancers. Each bell in the collection has its own pitch, and rings with a rich, gong-like sound.

The first sound on "We Are Interdependent" Ethno-Trance Dance is made by a single Kuling-Tang Bell. When working with instruments from the East, care must be taken to understand and integrate the different musical tonalities. For example, a bell marked "D" may actually correspond to a western D flat.

 Excerpt from Towards A Global Ethic: An Initial Declaration

"We are interdependent. Each of us depends on the well-being of the whole, and so we have respect for the community of living beings, for people, animals, and plants, and for the preservation of Earth, the air, water and soil."

Text reprinted with permission from CPWR.

We Are Interdependent ETHNO-TRANCE DANCE

Track 5 - 11:01

A music track for youth dance parties or music video projects

KULING-TANG

Instructions:

Translate
Find out what languages are represented by various project participants and their families. Collect translations of the phrase,

> "Each of us depends on the well-being of the whole".

Have participants practice pronouncing the line.

Prepare Artwork
Create illustrations on the theme in any large-format media, using translations of the words and/or the entire quotation.

Decorate the Dance Space
Make a bulletin board, banners, postcards, stage props, slideshows or other visual media; .

Create a Music Video
Using the CD soundtrack, make a music video adding movement, artwork, scenery, costumes and a script. Videotape, edit, and view the production. *(Note: Professional-level productions may require release forms for the performers, and public broadcast will require a video synchronization license from the publisher.)*

Composer's Notes:

"My son and I wrote this together when he was 20. He was enthused about dance parties and had several friends who were DJs. I was interested in how to connect positive themes with the teenage weekend dance scene. With the tragedy of the Columbine High School massacre in April of 1999, conversations started springing up about the impact of violent images in our media. On the inspirational side were groups like Earth Dance (an annual global dance party similar to Live-Aid) and the Techno-Cosmic Mass produced by Friends of Creation Spirituality in Oakland, CA."

Skills Involved	Age Group	Recommended Preparaton Time	Presentation Time
• singing • counting with feet • collecting and pronouncing multiple languages • art	3-5 6-10 11-14 15 to adult	4 weeks 3 weeks 2 weeks 1-2 weeks	5 to 10 minutes (5:08)

WE DECLARE! • We Are Interdependent (Ethno-Trance Dance) • Track 5

INDIGENOUS SHAKERS

Every culture in the world uses shakers of some sort in its native music, made from resilient natural materials found in each individual environment, such as sticks, gourds, pods, seeds, nutshells, seashells, pebbles, grasses, bones. Shakers from every continent are simple, creative, expressive noisemakers that the very young and the very old can create and play, with one or both hands.

a) a bent stick, a sliced gourd, and small seashells from Kenya, b) Palm Leaf Rattle from India, c, f, p) mini-gourds from Ghana, d) Ratatak from Ghana, e) ju-ju seeds from Ghana, g) shakeree from Ghana, h) Sistrum made from stick, wire and bottle caps (seen in Ancient Egyptian Heiroglyphics), j) carved, painted gourd from Peru, k) maracas from Mexico, l) painted gourd from Guatemala, m) leather, wood, feather with traditional Hopi Indian hand symbol (North America).

Opening Our Hearts

Track 6 - 3:09

An easy-to-perform song with simple choreography that is fun for any age group—from pre-schoolers to senior citizens— especially with added percussion instruments. It can be led by P.E. teachers or camp staff, or be used as an ice-breaker in an adult or family convening.

Instructions:

There are two ways to choreograph this piece, either honoring the four directions or the seven continents. Choose one.

The Four Directions

1. With chalk, tape, or symbolic objects, mark the floor or ground identifying points to represent North, South, East, and West.
2. Divide the group into four smaller groups. Each small group takes a position at one of the points.
3. Facing the center, all sing the first line of the song, "Opening our hearts to one another" adding hand gestures showing hands on the heart, then arms opening toward the center of the group. This line repeats three times.
4. Move into the center and join hands in a circle, sing the second line of the song, "together * * we can move mountains". This line repeats four times. On the beats following the word together (* *) step with the left foot, then the right. On the words "we can move mountains", lift hands up, still joined in the circle.
5. During the musical interlude, each segment of the group rotates clockwise to the next point of direction. For example, the group which started at the North moves to the point representing the East.
6. Repeat the song again, singing from a new position on the globe.
7. Repeat one more time. The group which began at the North will end up at the South.

CHA-CHAS
from Peru

Skills Involved	Age Group	Recommended Preparaton Time	Presentation Time
• singing • movement • arts/crafts* • awareness of place • knowledge of geography	3-5 6-10 11-14 15 to adult	2-4 weeks 2 weeks 1 week 1 week 20 minutes	5 to 10 minutes (5:08)

WE DECLARE! • Opening Our Hearts • Track 6

Opening Our Hearts

Choreography

The Seven Continents

1. On a large tarp, draw a twelve foot wide (at least) circle representing the globe.

2. Trace shapes of seven continents onto large poster board or other strong material.

3. Arrange the continents around the circle with the Pacific Ocean in the center.

4. Mark the Hawaiian Islands in the center of the circle.

5. Place indigenous instruments around the outside of the globe near the point of origin. For example, a Dijiri-doo could be close to the continent of Australia, *(see Sounds of the World for more details about adding instruments).*

6. Divide the group into two segments. One group will stand around the globe and provide instrumental rhythmic accompaniment. ("The Indigenous Peoples' Band").

7. Divide the other group into seven segments, assign each to a continent and select volunteers to be "Ambassadors". On the second line of the song, the "Ambassadors" hop to the Hawaiian Islands, then rotate to different continents.

8. Sing lines one and two with gestures and rotation between continents, as instructed in the description for the Four Directions.

Excerpt from Towards A Global Ethic: An Initial Declaration

"Opening our hearts to one another, we can move mountains."

Text reprinted with permission from the Parliament of the World's Religions (www.parliamentofreligions.org)

Teacher's Notes:

"Even though my group of kids this year was unruly and unfocused, this project was very successful, and enjoyable for everyone.

"The depth of learning, however, became clear to me at our Martin Luther King celebration. Two of the children, a boy and a girl, had written, 'I have a dream, that we open our hearts to one another.'"

—*Jim Costanzo, Piedmont Avenue Child Development Center*

We Declare!

Opening Our Hearts
Dedicated to Chris Ray Collins

Music © 1996 Merrill Collins

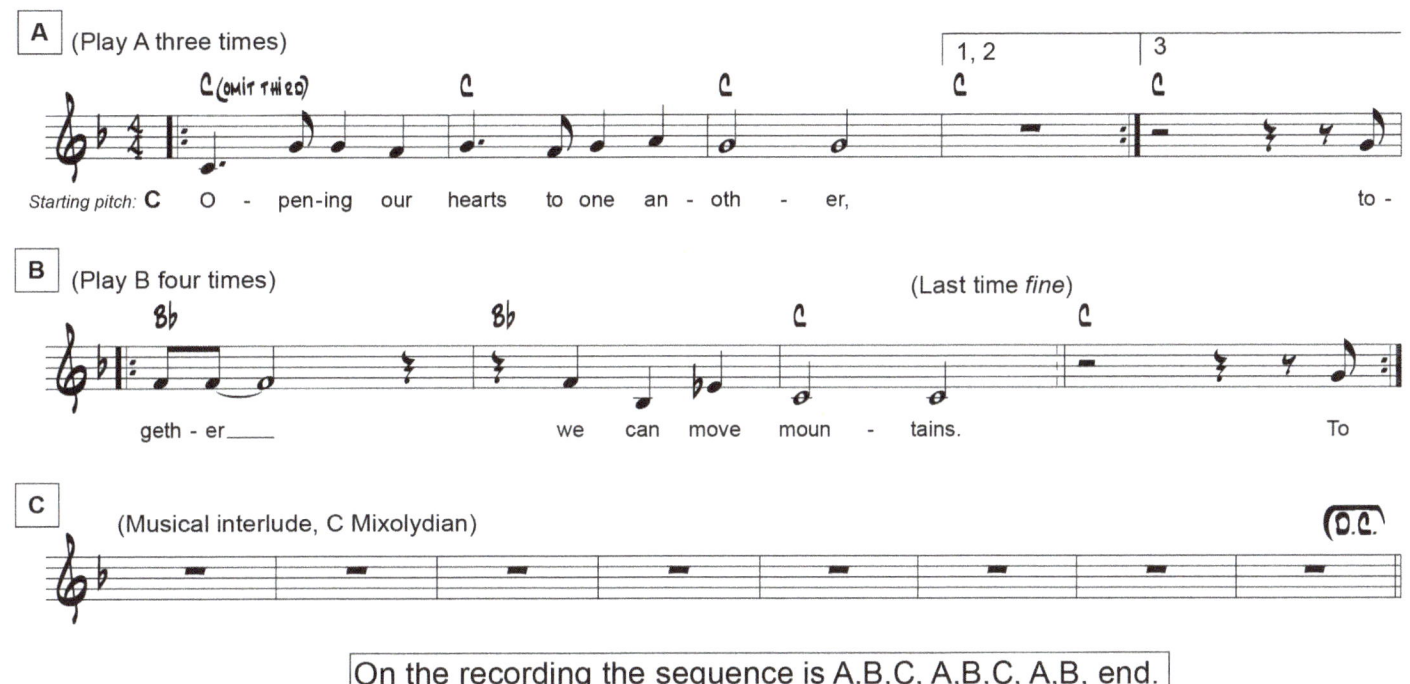

On the recording the sequence is A,B,C, A,B,C, A,B, end.

Text reprinted with permission from the Parliament of the World's Religions (www.parliamentofreligions.org)

DIN-DINS

The Din-Din (also called a Pancake Drum) is a type of shaker that makes noise by twisting it. Din-dins evolved independently on many continents.

Indigenous din-din from North America

Indigenous din-din from Asia

Indigenous din-din from Africa

SOUNDS OF THE WORLD

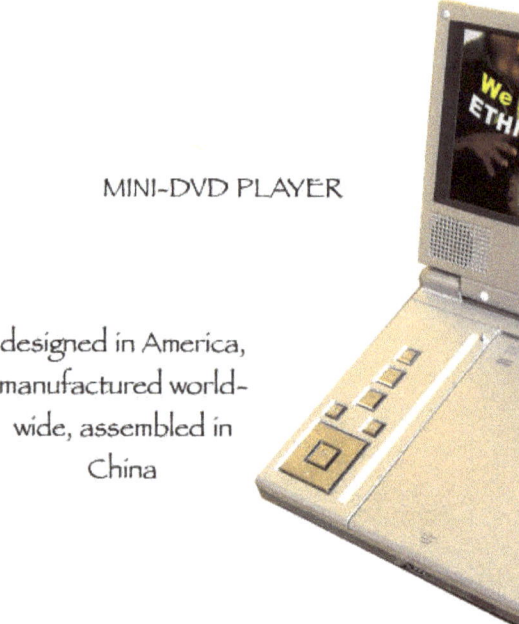

MINI-DVD PLAYER

designed in America, manufactured world-wide, assembled in China

MP3 PLAYER

MEDIA TECHNOLOGY
Since the beginning of time, music has been a live cultural expression of people coming together in song, dance, and instrumentation. Media technology in the last century has created multiple ways to document culture, offering passive ways to listen and watch. Technology has also added ways people can actively create, collect, compile, and edit their own media files.

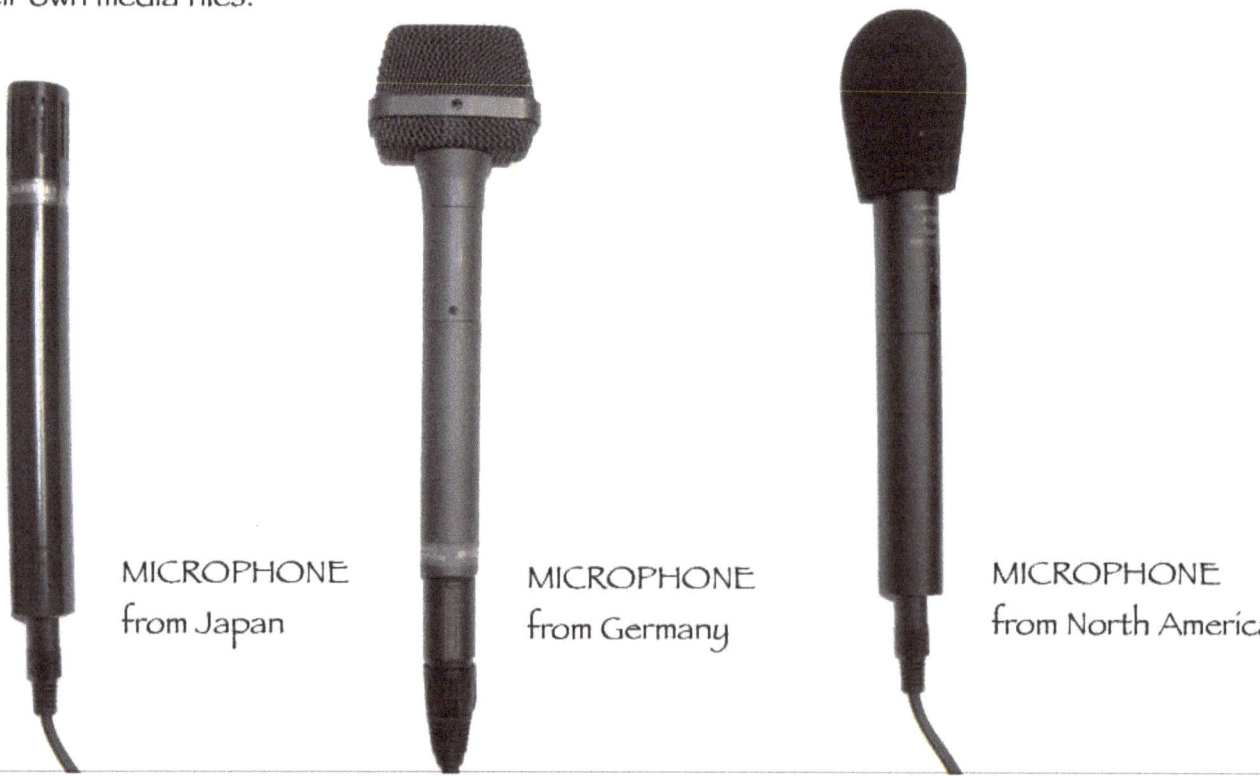

MICROPHONE from Japan

MICROPHONE from Germany

MICROPHONE from North America

We, the Peoples PUBLIC SERVICE ANNOUNCEMENTS

Tracks 7-13 ~1:00 ea.

This audio or video project involves whatever technology is available to the group to create 60-second "commercials" to teach and promote ethical values.

Instructions:

Select an excerpt and record it over the music on the soundtrack. Memorize as is, or explore putting into your own words. Discuss or pursue ways of broadcasting the segments via public access TV, podcasts, school or local radio stations.

One or more of the following excerpts from *Towards A Global Ethic: An Initial Declaration* may be read over the music.

Each excerpt may also be followed by a quote or reading.

We Are Interdependent (Track 7)
"We are interdependent. Each of us depends on the well-being of the whole, and so we have respect for the community of living beings, for people, animals, and plants, and for the preservation of Earth, the air, water and soil."

Cause and Effect (Track 8)
"We take individual responsibility for all we do. All our decisions, actions, and failures to act have consequences."

Golden Rules (Track 9)
"We must treat others as we wish others to treat us. We make a commitment to respect life and dignity, individuality and diversity, so that every person is treated humanely, without exception. We must have patience, and acceptance. We must be able to forgive, learning from the past but never allowing ourselves to be enslaved by memories of hate. Opening our hearts to one another, we must sink our narrow differences for the cause of the world community, practicing a culture of solidarity and relatedness."

Humankind is our Family (Track 10)
" We consider humankind our family. We do not live for ourselves alone, but also serving others, never forgetting the children, the aged, the poor, the suffering, the disabled, the refugees, and the lonely. Humankind is our family."

Forsaking Violence (Track 11)
"We commit ourselves to a culture of non-violence, respect, justice, and peace. We shall not oppress, injure, torture, or kill other human beings, forsaking violence as a means of settling differences. Make a just and peaceful world, with nature-friendly ways of life."

Opening Our Hearts (Track 12)
"Opening our hearts to one another, together we can move mountains."

Text reprinted with permission from the Parliament of the World's Religions

Every Man, Woman, and Child (Track 13)*
"Give every man, woman, and child our human rights."
*this bonus track is from the song, Every Man,Woman, and Child, which is a musical setting of the **Universal Declaration of Human Rights**. More info can be found in Every Man, Woman and Child (see back cover).

Composer's Notes:

"We are bombarded with media every day, so it can be empowering to create our own. In exploring ways to educate children, youth and adults about the concepts of the global ethic, this was my first creative recording project. I asked friends and family to practice speaking a favorite paragraph from the Global Ethic document over the music as if they were a radio or TV spokesperson. In the early days of the internet, we posted these free sound bi s for use by radio stations and for use as internet postcards."

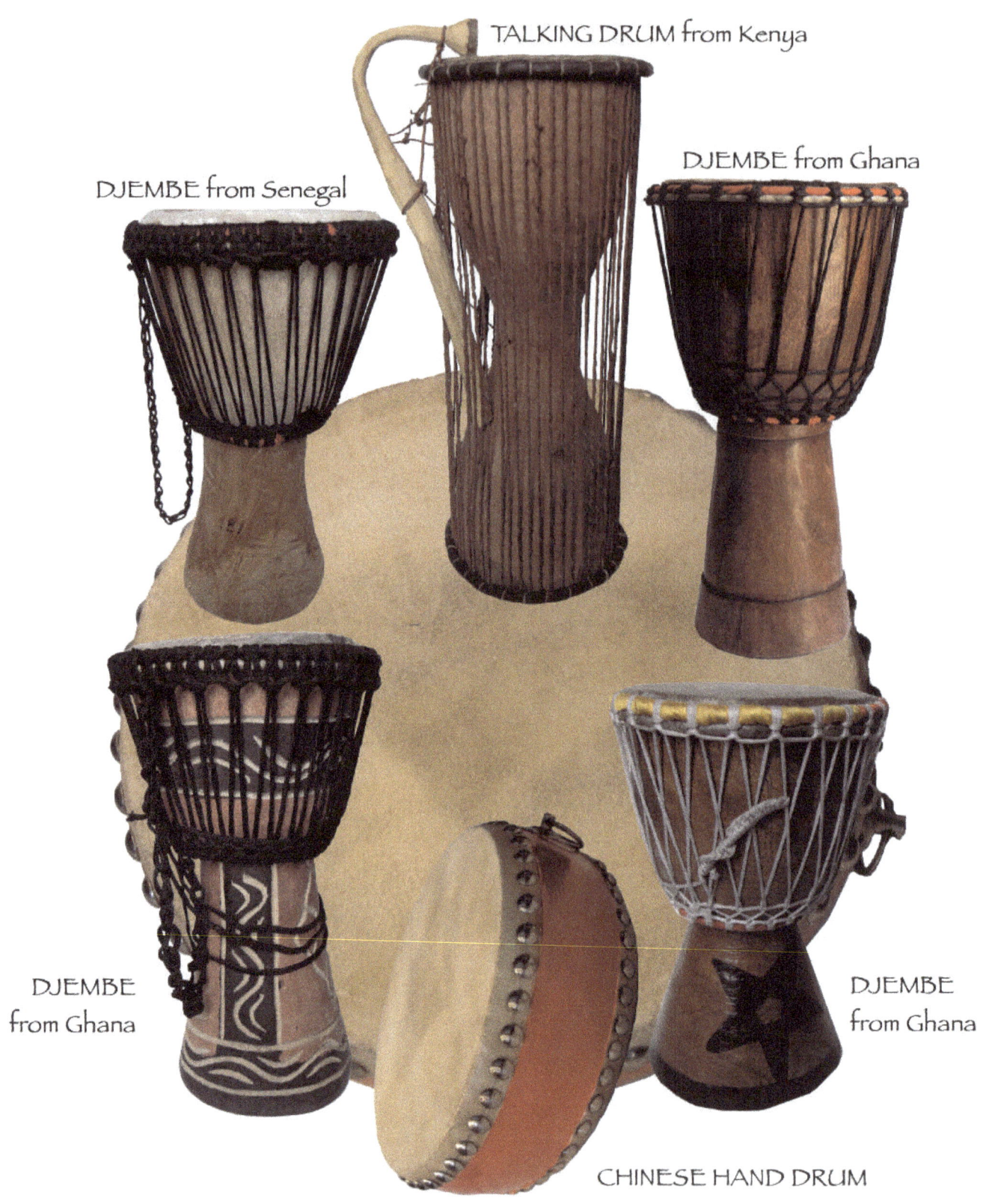

SOUNDS OF THE WORLD

Cause and Effect

Refer to Track 8 for an example

This rhythmic piece is especially suitable for youth who are naturally expressive and like to improvise with rap/spoken word and explore beats.

Instructions:

Forming a Drum Circle

Each person holds a hand drum of any size. Sitting in a circle, each person takes a turn leading the rest of the group in a rhythm.

1) Each drummer makes up their own short rhythm. The other drummers repeat it back.

2) Each person speaks the words "Cause and Effect" to go with a rhythm. The others repeat it back.

3) Freestyle. Speak a part of the phrase only; add other spoken words to emphasize it. Create causes and effects with voice, the timbres of drums, or body-beats.

Creative Writing

Assign each participant a four-sentence verse telling a story on the theme of the quote. It can be about a real or imaginary event, in which the consequences of decisions, actions, or failures to act become obvious. Practice speaking the words over a drum beat, trying different ways to place the verbal accents. In this way the piece is what has been called "onomatopoeia", demonstrating the cause and effect theme through rhythmic verbal as well as instrumental means.

DRUM
on lattice stand
from Senegal

Skills Involved	Age Group	Recommended Preparaton Time	Presentation Time
• Creating beat patterns • Playing hand drums • Creative writing • Listen and repeat • Spoken word or rap	3-5 6-10 11-14 15 to adult	1 week 1 week 1 week 2 weeks	10 to 20 minutes

WE DECLARE! • *Cause and Effect* • Track 8

Cause and Effect

Lyrics

In this particular piece, the spoken lyrics are "cause and effect," but the drums do some talking of their own. This is a great piece for Hip-Hop artists.

 Excerpt from Towards A Global Ethic: An Initial Declaration

"We take individual responsibility for all we do. All our decisions, actions, and failures to act have consequences."

Text reprinted with permission from the Parliament of the World's Religions (www.parliamentofreligions.org)

THE TALKING DRUM

The talking drum has heads on both ends which are connected by leather cords. When the drummer holds the drum under his arm and squeezes it, he changes pressure on the cords, and thus changes the pitch of the heads. The smallest ones are called "gan gan", and the largest are called "dun dun."

Drums have often symbolized political power in west African communities such as Yoruba, and skilled drummers ("onigangan") have held considerable status.

Talking drums seem even to have their own language, as they can closely imitate the rhythms and intonations of human speech. The sounds of talking drums can carry rhythms or messages for miles. A religion that cherishes the spirit of the drums spread from Nigeria and Ghana to South and Central America, the Caribbean and the United States during the slave trade. Talking drums were banned in the U.S. because they were believed capable of inciting rebellion.

Talking drums can be heard as part of "juju" music, which has its roots in traditional Yoruba music.

TALKING DRUM from Ghana

We Declare!

Cause and Effect Chant

Examples of Possible Rhythms:

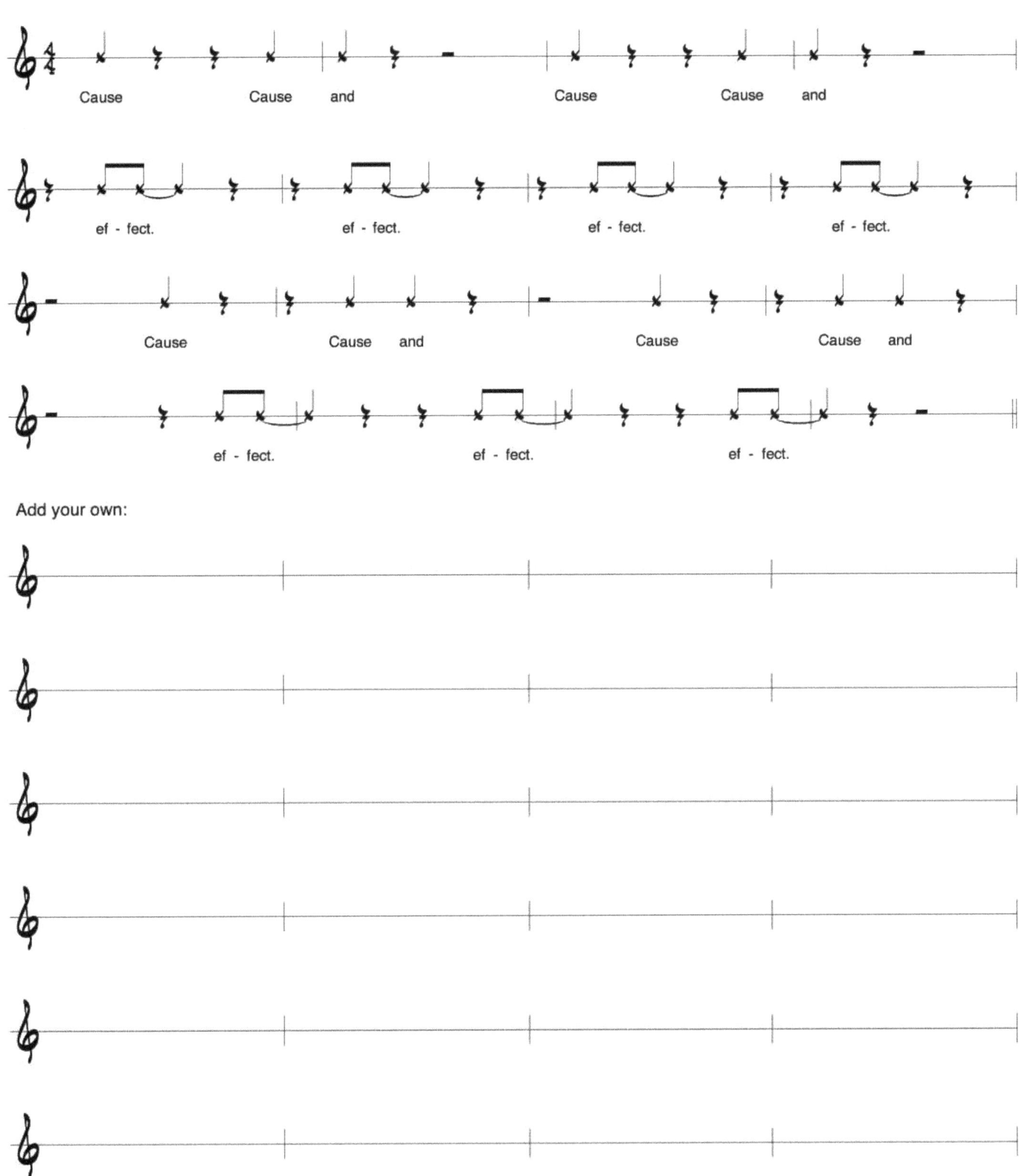

Add your own:

WE DECLARE! • Cause and Effect • Score

SOUNDS OF THE WORLD

Tracks 1, 3, 5, 7, 10 and 13 on the We Declare CD feature Charles Moselle playing bansuri flutes.

BANSURI FLUTES

Made in India, this is a bamboo open-holed flute unlike the silver flute of Western music in several respects. Bansuris are individually made in different keys. Therefore a bansuri player needs a collection of Bansuris in order to accommodate various tonalities. It is easy to "bend notes," or find the pitches in between the pitches which are "fixed" on the modern piano. A bansuri flute is more like a voice, and like the vocal styles of the East.

Appendicies

I	**Global Ethic Resources**	31
II	**World Instrument Resources**	32
III	**How to Use the Instrumental Soundtrack**	33
IV	**Release for Video Documentation**	34

MARIMBA
from Guatemala

Appendix I

Global Ethic Resources
For further learning

Parliament of the World's Religions
www.parliamentofreligions.org

70 East Lake Street, Suite 230
Chicago, Illinois 60601
U.S.A.

Towards a Global Ethic: An Initial Declaration
www.parliamentofreligions.org/Global-Ethic-Declaration

To endorse the Global Ethic document, visit:
www.parliamentofreligions.org/globalethic/endorse-global-ethic/

Global Ethic Institute
Hintere Grabenstraße 26
72070 Tübingen
Germany
Telefon +49 7071 54940-30
Fax +49 7071 54940-40

Temple of Understanding
777 U.N. Plaza 3E
New York, NY 10017
www.templeofunderstanding.org/

Appendix II

World Percussion Instruments
Where to Buy ~ Where to Learn More

Building an instrument collection is a special pleasure. When shopping for world percussion instruments, please be mindful about fair trade, which helps artisans keep their cultures alive around the world. Instruments make wonderful souvenirs, but there are many import companies that bring them to you. Call and ask your local music stores or fair trade import stores, or search and order online. Try search words such as: percussion instruments, world percussion instruments, bells, shakers, hand drums, rainsticks, singing bowls, etc.

HOW TO MAKE RAIN STICKS:
kinderart.com/art-lessons/multic/rainsticks/
www.enchantedlearning.com/crafts/music/rainstick/

HOW TO PLAY SINGING BOWLS:
Singing Bowls*: A Practical Handbook of Instruction and Use* by Eva Rudy Jansen (Binkey Kok Publications)

Whale-shaped WOOD BLOCK from Thailand

Thank you to the following Bay Area stores for the use of images of your beautiful instruments:

- **Global Exchange** *(pages 2, 10, 20, 22)*
- **Clarion Music** *(inside cover and pages ii, iv, v, 2, 6, 7, 11, 14, 15, 18, 19, 26, 27, 33)*
- **What the Traveler Saw** *(Gankoqui, shown on page 3)*
- **Gathering Tribes** *(Hopi rattle, shown on page 20)*
- **Kathmandu Imports** *(inside cover and pages i, 6, and 17)*
- **Onyx & Opal** *(pages 20, 26, 28)*
- **Hear Music** *(Castanet, shown on page iii)*

WE DECLARE! • Appendices

Appendix III

How to Use
The Soundtrack Recordings

Listen on Spotify *Purchase on iTunes* *Purchase on Amazon*

Use as a Soundtrack
For a live performance, purchase the MP3 online and add it to your performance playlist. Rehearse using your sound system. Mic the vocalists and don't forget to do a sound-check on the volume balance before the performance!

Background Listening
Use the recorded instrumental music for background listening as children or adults are working on other aspects of the project. This not only helps them relax and focus on their work, it helps performers visualize themselves ahead of time, and helps memorize the tunes.

Special Instructions for Non-Musicians:

A few basic rhythm terms:
- **a beat** = a basic unit of rhythm; a pulse.
- **a measure** = a group of beats
- **time signature** = the numbers at the beginning of the score. The top number shows how many beats are in each measure.

How to count the introduction of the song:
Count each measure (**1**, 2, 3, 4; **2**, 2, 3, 4; **3**, 2, 3, 4; etc.) with movement of feet, fingers, or hands or using added percussion. On the vocal scores, the numbers tell how many measures of introductory music lead up to the place where the singing starts.

For example:
We Are Interdependent, is in 4/4 time. To count the 14 measure introduction, count 4 beats 14 times. "**1**, 2, 3, 4—**2**, 2, 3, 4—**3**, 2, 3, 4—**4**, 2, 3, 4," etc.

Golden Rules, is in 6/8 time. To count the 8 measure introduction, count 6 beats 8 times. "**1**, 2, 3,4,5,6—**2**, 2,3, 4, 5,6—**3**, 2, 3,4,5,6," etc.

How to find the Pitch
To find the first note of each song go to a keyboard and use the image below. If there is no keyboard available, a pitch pipe can be used.

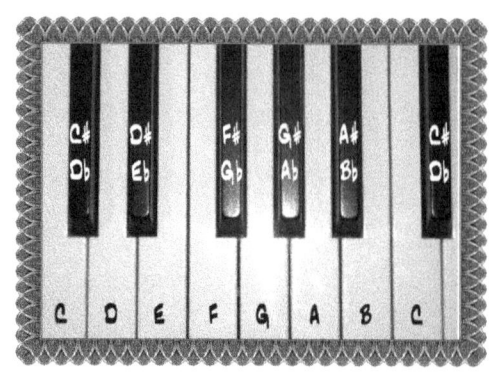

Starting notes:
We Are Interdependent:	F
Golden Rules Ceremony:	A
Forsaking Violence:	E
Humankind is Our Family:	F
Opening Our Hearts:	C
Every Man, Woman, and Child:	F

Appendix IV

Release for Video Documentation
for minors and general participants

Organizer: _____

_____

Participant Name: _____

Program Title: _____

Event Hosts: _____

Date: _____

Participation: _____

Fee: _____

I have participated as indicated on the above program ("The Program"). For value received, I hereby grant permission to you to utilize my appearance in the Program in any and all manner and media throughout the world in perpetuity.

I agree that my participation in the Program may be edited in according to your sole discretion. I consent to the use of my name, likeness, voice and biographical material about me in connection with production, advertising and promotional purposes. I expressly release you, your agents, employees, licensees and assigns from all claims which I have or may have for invasion of privacy, defamation or any other cause of action arising out of production, duplication, broadcast or exhibition of any appearance.

Signature: _____ Date: _____

Address: _____ Phone: _____

_____

If Participant is legally a minor in the state where he/she resides, sign below:

I, (print name), _____ hereby represent and warrant that I am a parent (or guardian) of the minor who has signed the above release, and I hereby agree that we shall both be bound thereby.

Signed: _____ Date: _____

Address: _____ Phone: _____

_____

Index

Africa 22
America (see North America)
Ani-Hu 7
Asia 22
Australia 18
Bansuri Flutes 30
Bell Tree 15
Bells cover, inside back cover, i, 2, 3, 14, 18
Bolivia 2
Brass Bells inside back cover, 2, 6
Castanet ii
Cause and Effect 27
Cha-Chas 2, 21
Chile 6
China 6, 26
Chinese Bells © page
Chinese Hand Drum 26
Cowbells 14
Dijiri-Doo 18
Din-Dins 22
Djembe 26
Dragonfly 10
Drums 26, 27, 28
Duck 10
Dumbec 35
DVD player 24
Egg Shaker 20
Egypt 20
Elephant Bells 2
Fish v, 32
Flutes iv, 10, 31
Forsaking Violence 11, 25
Frog 10
Gankoqui 3
Germany 24
Ghana 3, 20, 26, 28
Ghungaroo 1
Glass Harmonica 14
Global Ethic Document v, 1
Goat hooves 2
Golden Rules Ceremony 7, 25
Gong 11
Gourds 20
Grasshopper 36
Guatemala 20, 31
Hopi 20
Hu 7, 16
Humankind is Our Family 15, 25
India inside front cover, iv, 1, 2, 6,
   11, 20, 14
Indonesia 11
Initial Declaration Towards a Global Ethic, The 1
iPod 24
Japan 15, 22, 24

Ju-ju seeds 20
Kenya 20, 26
Kuling-Tang 18, 19
Lattice Drum 27
Maracas 20
Mexico 10, 20
Microphones 24
Nicaragua 10
North America iv, 20, 22, 24
Ocarina 10, 31
Opening Our Hearts 20, 25
Palm Leaf Rattle inside front cover, 20
Pancake Drums 23
Peace Flute iv
Peru 20, 21
Phillipines 18
Rain Sticks 6
Rasp 10, 36
Ratatak 20
Rattles (see Shakers)
Senegal 26
Shakere 20
Shakers 2, 20
Singing Bowl title page, 17
Sistrum 20
South America 6
Spain iii
Talking Drum 28, 35
Thailand v, 32
Tibet title page, i, 6, 17
Tingsha 6
Turtle 31
Vietnam ii, 10, 35
We Are Interdependent 3, 19, 25
We Are Interdependent - Ethno-Trance Dance 19, 24
We The Peoples Public Service Announcements 25
Woodblock ii, v, 32 inside front cover

Grasshopper RASP from Vietnam

The Composer

Merrill Collins began writing and performing usic in early childhood, with the encouragement of a family of artists, musicians and inventors. From the age of twelve, Merrill worked as an accompanist for vocalists and dancers in the metropolitan area of NYC. Working her way through college as a musician, Merrill earned a Master of Music Degree from the SF Conservatory of Music on a full scholarship.

In addition to concert performances, Merrill worked for 17 years as Senior Musician in the University of California in Berkeley's Department of Theater, Dance, and Performance Studies. Her diversity of musical styles has roots there, having played for master classes by the Alvin Ailey Dance Co., Mark Morris Co., Joe Goode, Janice Garrett, Frank Shawl, Josie Moselie, as well as a series of collaborations with Duncan Dancer Mary Sano.

While raising her son Chris Ray, Merrill created music and community service projects for Montessori schools, YMCA School Age Child Care programs, private, parochial, and public schools. With Avon Mattison, she developed a human rights curricula that became the Pathways to Peace model for children's peace education still in use today with the United Nations. Multimedia pieces and humanitarian projects which were produced internationally later became published as the We Agree! music books that teach about key world agreements: the Universal Declaration of Human Rights, the U.N. Convention on the Rights of the Child, and Toward a Global Ethic: An Initial Declaration.

Through her music, Merrill's heart-centered voice for global harmony and humanist evolution has resonated with listeners worldwide. She produced performances of original work for many major events and broadcasts, including the 50th Anniversary of the United Nations, UNCHR Human Rights Day, Amnesty International, United Way, UN World Habitat Day, Earth Day. Her works have been produced on Austrian national television and E-TV in Capetown South Africa, where her works were cited as "Gifts of Service to the World." Her production of Minute of Silence was featured in three languages in a global broadcast for the International Day of Peace. Merrill received two Global Peace Song Awards for the Chant and Hip-Hop versions of her composition "Every Man, Woman, and Child," which were included on the 2017 Project Peace on Earth compilation.

Merrill played in the Music Healing Department of Cedars-Sinai Hospital in Beverly Hills, and her music was also studied at the Cousins Center at UCLA for its positive impact in T'ai Chi classes offered as treatment for people with anxiety and insomnia. As a member of the Sound Healers Association and a voting member of the Grammy Foundation (NARAS), Merrill is interested in the benefits of music on all forms of healing, including Qigong, Yoga, deep breathing, meditation, and contemplation. Merrill is a voting member of the Grammy Foundation (NARAS), and her volumes of neoclassical piano music in collaboration with world class artists can be found on www.spiralingmusic.com, as well as on her live music site, www.merrillcollinsmusic.com.

Merrill's video collaborations with her husband, photographer Yvon Chausseblanche, can be seen on Youtube. She is available for live presentations and performances in the San Francisco Bay area, where she and Yvon enjoy their two grandchildren.

The Artists

Merrill Collins, *composer, producer, author, performer: keyboards, bells* • Pope Flyne, *African Drum* • Joseph Hebert, *'cello* •
Chris Ray Collins, *dijiri-do, drums* • Jeff Dunn, *marimba, percussion* • Charles Moselle, *shakahachi, bansuri flute*
Lizzy Cole, Chris Ray Collins, Dan Ross, Merrill Collins, *vocals* on Golden Rules • Daryl Keyes, *vocals* on Cause and Effect •
Cause and Effect co-produced by Daryl Keyes • *We Are Interdependent* ethno-trance dance co-produced by Chris Ray Collins.
Graphic design by Kristen Caven and Fatima Yousuf • Score design by Karl Pister • Photography by Yvon Chausseblanche.

www.ingramcontent.com/pod-product-compliance
Lightning Source LLC
Chambersburg PA
CBHW042315300426
44110CB00043B/2959